"a" is for **Advertise!**

JoAnn is in charge of advertising for the Bake Sale. Her checklist includes:

★ Make up eye-catching posters and fliers ～ be sure all the important information is included, like date, time, location and who the sponsor is. Let readers know what a good cause you're working for and how the proceeds will be put to good use.

Bake Sale TODAY!

★ Distribute flyers to everyone you know, and encourage others to spread the news ～ *word·of·mouth is good and free!*

Bake Sale →

... Yadda Yadda Yadda ...

★ Check out different ways to publicize your event : radio, newspapers, television, school & church bulletins... all sometimes give free ad space as a community service.

GeT the WORD OUT!

BAKE SALE SATURDAY JAN. 21

③

"b" is for

Bake!

Mary Elizabeth is the Baking Director. What does she do?

★ It's fine to have a wide variety of goodies. Find out who makes terrific fudge.... who won the blue ribbon for apple pie at last year's fair... ask people to bring their favorites. And it's a great idea to offer some sugar-free desserts!

★ Decide who's gonna make what. Whether your sale is a casually planned event ("Holly, bring us something baked....") or choreographed to the last detail ("Vickie, please make 4 dozen bar cookies, maybe apricot....") it's nice to know what the final count will be on bake-sale day.

sugar free cake

★ Explore the possibility of offering samples of the delicious baked goods... small slices of breads, broken cookies, a sliver of fudge. Once they taste it, how can they resist?

Be our Guest!

Plan.

Hmmm....

④

the Country Friends collection

Bake Sales

Kate...
spent $127 at
the sale.

Mary
Elizabeth...
baked 127 brownies.

BAKE
SALE

Holly
...hand-colored
127 Bake Sale signs.

Raise Funds and Fun

with a wonderful **Country Friends®** style **BAKe SALE!**

got a worthy cause? get organized and get baking!

"c" is for

Creativity!

★ Make your Bake Sale so much fun that people <u>want</u> to get involved! Have a group Baking Party... Let your kids help decorate the packages...and mix dough...even help at the Sales Table. (Little kids are often irresistable salespeople.)

Wanna Buy a cookie, mister?

Vickie is delegated the Creative Duties for the event. She'll be busy!

★ Dream up a great idea to attract buyers to the Bake Sale table.... perhaps a demonstration of cake decorating? Let people garnish their own cookies with sprinkles and frosting... Personalize gingerbread boys and girls with names in icing...

★ Think up an idea or theme to build the Bake Sale around. For instance, a Valentines Day Sale might be called "Heartwarmers" or "Sweet Hearts" then tie all your baking & packaging ideas to that theme by using red and white ribbons... heart-shaped-cookies...valentines for tags.

Be different!

25¢

for You ♥

"d" is for

Display!

★ Find fun ways to package your baked goodies without breaking the bank.

Pack cookies in gift-wrapped potato chip cans... bake bread in a foil-lined clay pot... Use stickers to decorate cellophane bags... stencil plain old brown paper sacks to hold a dozen oatmeal cookies.

Remember, the pretty packages help sell the stuff!

Holly is our Display wizard. Her imagination will be in overdrive for this spectacular Bake Sale!

COOKIES

★ Bake sale tables look great covered in something creative: A spring sale table decorated with a pretty floral sheet ... warm stadium blankets thrown over an autumn sale table... colorful quilts (washable ones!) in winter, cool stripes on a summer tablecloth... all help set the mood. Use homey props for your display, too: a stoneware kitchen bowl full of individually wrapped brownies... a basket of gingersnaps in a bandana-wrap.

Entertain!

★ Recruit a volunteer to bring a little L*I*F*E to your sale. Do you know a guitar-strummer or a harmonica player? Can you bribe the church choir to sing for a cookie or two? Anybody who can help you attract a crowd to your table is your friend, so don't be shy in asking local talent to help!

Kate is responsible for making the Bake Sale a successful, entertaining event.

★ Give away a fortune with every homemade cookie ("I see a tall, dark man who loves Buckeye cookies in your future... better buy more!")... just print them out on your computer, and tape them to the packages. Give your customers something extra that doesn't cost much ⌒ make them feel like they are getting their money's worth ⌒ make 'em happy!

★ Don't think of it as a Bake Sale ⌒ think PARTY, only with guests BUYING their own refreshments! At a Halloween Bake Sale, ask your helpers to dress in costume. If your sale is around Christmas-time, let the kids wear elf clothes!

SALE

Have FUN!

Dress-up Details:

INEXPENSIVE & CLEVER PACKAGING INSPIRATIONS

★ Watch at tag sales for old & interesting single plates. You can often find a real treasure for pennies to fill full of yummies at the next bake sale!

(JUST THINK OF IT: A BAKE SALE TABLE COVERED WITH AN OLD LACE TABLECLOTH, AND ALL THE GOODIES ARE OFFERED ON VINTAGE CHINA PLATES! WOW!)

★ Paper doilies are a bake-saler's best friend! Lay one on a styrofoam or paper plate under chocolate cake... fold one under - and - around the sides of a loaf of bread before sliding it in a plastic bag.

★ Check out your neighborhood paper and party stores for cheap-but-fun treat sacks, Chinese food cartons, French-fry boxes and more.

⑧

The fine art of wrapping (on·the·cheap)

Have fun & be ingenious, but remember that customers will want to SEE the food they're buying under those oh-so-clever wrappings!

★ Slide unusual containers & open boxes of baked goods into clear cello bags ～ buyers can peep inside to see the goodies. Your neighborhood bakery may have those wonderful, crispy cello bags to sell ～ ask! Food looks so good in those shiny wonders.

★ Wrap 2 or 3 big cookies in clear food wrap, then gather colored tulle around them and tie with curling ribbon. Make a whole basket-full; people will buy them as little take-along gifts.

Most ideas are Step-by Step Children of Other ideas.

—A.F.OSBORN— 9

Entertaining Bake Sale TAGS

"It's ODD but it just might work..."

Everybody knows that half the fun of getting a present is in the unwrapping... and sometimes the silly card is as good as the gift! So wrap your bake sale goodies in a memorable fashion ⌒ and go ahead! Add that silly card! Here are a few ideas to get you started:

To eat or not to eat, that is the question.

FOUR SCORE AND SEVEN COOKIES AGO, OUR BAKE SALE MOTHERS BROUGHT FORTH UPON THIS SCHOOL GROUND A NEW BATCH OF BROWNIES, CONCEIVED IN THE KITCHEN AND DEDICATED TO MAKING ENOUGH MONEY TO BUY NEW SOCCER BALLS.

an apple pie every day will keep the doctor away.

Try writing a little poem to go with each treat ⌒ it doesn't have to make sense, it just has to make your buyers

Smile!

Who knows? Butter, eggs & chocolate chips might be the way to skinny hips.

Tag it... bright and beautiful!

★ If someone in your bake sale group is especially talented in wrapping or is clever with her hands, ask her to take charge of wrapping and tagging the baked goods— maybe she'll have an eye-catching idea for coordinating all the different goodies for a pretty table.

I'm thinking gold ribbons and calligraphy

★ Hand out a blank recipe card to all the bakers for each sale package — have them complete the cards for a great tie-on tag!

Vickie's Apple Turnovers

★ Arts & crafts stores have a super selection of neat papers in all kinds of patterns — use specialty scissors to cut cool edges on your tags, then dress 'em up with rubber stamped designs.

★ Use bright & beautiful ribbons to tie on the price tags — or knot on something different like a scrap of homespun, a piece of twine and a sprig of evergreen or a length of tulle netting.

You'll love our Oatmeal Cookies!

⑪

Home · baked for You!

Fill 'Er Up!
homemade

Cookies

---

for your cookie jar

Nothing's Better Than
home ♥ made

♥ ...something sweet... ♥ ...a bake sale treat ♥

Help yourself!

Simply take this page down to the local copy machine. Run off a bunch of copies on heavy paper and cut 'em out... voilá! Bake Sale Tags!

(HINT: IF YOU TURN THE TAGS AND MAKE AN EXTRA COPY... THEN DO A LITTLE JUDICIOUS CUTTING & PASTING... YOU SHOULD BE ABLE TO GET (6) TAGS OUT OF EVERY 8½"x11" COPY!)

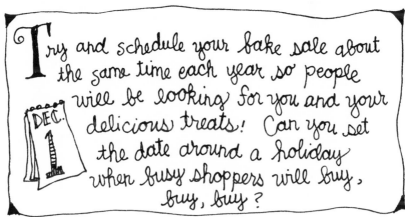

Try and schedule your bake sale about the same time each year so people will be looking for you and your delicious treats! Can you set the date around a holiday when busy shoppers will buy, buy, buy?

DEC. 1

Every production must resemble its author. —MIGUEL DE CERVANTES

⑬

They'll Line Up to Buy...

Butterscotch Polka Dots

a recipe from
Ria Ann Rigby

★ Malta, ID

18·¼ oz box chocolate
    cake mix
½ c. vegetable oil

2 eggs
2 c. butterscotch chips
½ c. walnuts, chopped

Combine cake mix, oil and eggs in mixing bowl. Stir in butterscotch chips and walnuts. Drop by rounded tablespoons onto ungreased cookie sheet. Bake at 350 degrees for 8 to 10 minutes or until centers are just set. Let stand 2 minutes. Remove from pan and let cool completely. Makes 3 dozen.

Those nifty plastic salad boxes from your grocery store deli make great cookie containers. Lay colored tissue in one, then layer cookies on it. Pretty!

Buckeyes

a recipe from
Debbie Lloyd

* Newark, OH

2 c. peanut butter
½ c. butter, softened
1 t. vanilla extract
1 lb. powdered sugar

12-oz. pkg. semi-sweet
chocolate chips

In a large mixing bowl, mix peanut butter, butter and vanilla together. Add powdered sugar a small amount at a time, mixing by hand. Continue to add powdered sugar until mixture is able to be rolled into small balls that stay together. Melt chocolate in double boiler. Place toothpicks into balls ~ dip into chocolate. Place balls onto wax paper-lined cooked sheet. Place in cool area or freezer to set. Makes 4 to 5 dozen.

...and Buy some More!

Brown * Eyed Susans

a recipe
from Terri Demidovich

* Charleston, SC

1 c. margarine
2 c. plus ¼ c. sugar, divided
½ t. almond extract
2 c. all-purpose flour
½ t. salt
½ c. butter

2 sq. semi-sweet chocolate
¼ c. light corn syrup
½ c. sweetened condensed milk
1 t. vanilla
Garnish: 60 almonds

Cream margarine and ¼ cup sugar until light and fluffy; blend in extract. Add flour and salt; mix well. Shape rounded teaspoons of dough into balls. Place on ungreased cookie sheet and flatten slightly. Bake at 375 degrees for 10 to 12 minutes. Cool. Prepare frosting by melting butter and chocolate in a saucepan; blend in remaining sugar, corn syrup and condensed milk. Boil for 2 minutes. Remove from heat. Add vanilla and stir well. Frost cookies and top with almonds. Makes 4 to 5 dozen.

Bake a Bunch!

Old Favorite Easy Peanut Butter Cookies

a recipe
from
Sammy Polizzi-Morrison   ★ Aurora, Co

1 c. sugar
1 c. peanut butter
1 egg
1 t. baking soda

Mix all ingredients together. Form into 8 to 10 balls and place on an ungreased baking sheet. Bake at 350 degrees for 15 minutes. Makes 8 to 10 big cookies.

Save those green plastic cartons strawberries come in ~ thread colored streamers through the holes in the sides and drop a plastic bag full of cookies in the basket!

I'm extraordinarily **PATIENT** provided I get my own way in the end.
~ MARGARET THATCHER

BAKE SALE →

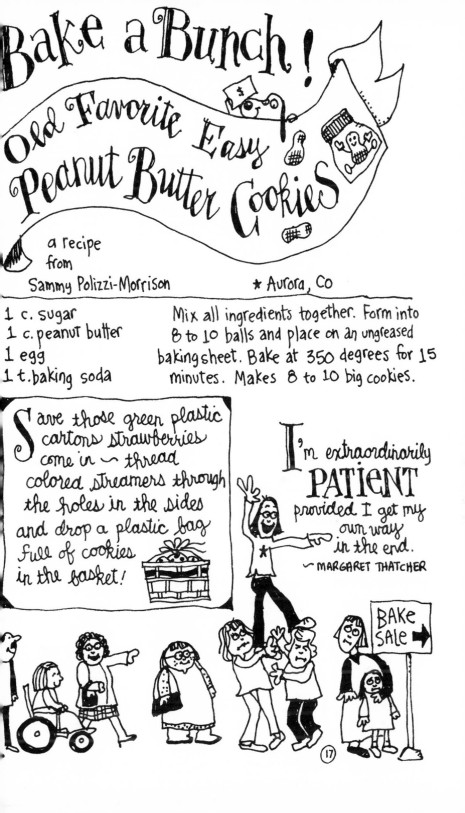

CHOCOLATE CHIP COOKIES

I dub thee...

...*king of cookies*.

a recipe from
Roseann Haley   ★ Cutler, In.

2 c. brown sugar, packed
2 c. shortening
2 t. baking soda
1 T. vanilla extract
4 eggs
4·⅓ c. all·purpose flour
12·oz. pkg. chocolate chips

Preheat oven to 350 degrees. In a large bowl, mix together all ingredients. Drop by spoonful onto greased cookie sheet. Bake about 10 minutes or until slightly browned. Makes 2 dozen cookies.

Keep a cooler of ice·cold milk in pint·size cartons on the sale table by the chocolate chip cookies for an add·on sale nobody can resist.

MOO MILK

Oatmeal Raisin Cookies

a recipe from
Judy Haller   ★ Dover, DE

Who can say "no"?

2 sticks butter, softened
1 c. sugar
1 c. brown sugar, packed
2 eggs
2 c. instant oatmeal
2 c. corn flake cereal
2 c. all-purpose flour
4 t. vanilla extract
1 t. baking powder
1 t. baking soda
1 to 2 c. raisins

In big bowl, mix all ingredients. Drop by teaspoonfuls on greased cookie sheet. Bake at 350 degrees for 15 minutes. Makes 3 to 4 dozen cookies.

Sell "singles" at your sale for those who just can't wait!

HURRY UP:

Double·Quicky Chocolate Nuggets

Hello?
Hello? Mary Elizabeth?
This is Joan down at the school... did Molly remember to tell you to bring 78 dozen cookies to the bake sale?

Today? Now, they need to be wrapped and
...
and
...
and
...
see you by 8:30, ok?

a recipe from Ann Fehr   ★ Trappe, PA

18·¼ oz. box chocolate cake mix
¼ c. oil
1 egg
½ c. chocolate chips

*

Combine cake mix, oil and egg; stir in chocolate chips. Drop teaspoonfuls 2 inches apart onto a greased cookie sheet. Bake at 350 degrees for 10 to 12 minutes. Makes 4 dozen.

Keep ingredients for a quick-bake goodie on hand at all times so you'll be ready-to-roll at a moment's notice!

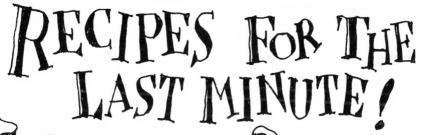

RECIPES FOR THE LAST MINUTE!

Triple Fudge Brownies

Take it warm, right out of the oven!

a recipe from
Janine Edwards   ★ Hulett, WY

3.½ oz. pkg. instant chocolate pudding
2.½ c. chocolate cake mix
12·oz. pkg. chocolate chips

*

Prepare pudding according to package directions; quickly whisk in cake mix & chips. Pour into an 8" square lightly oiled baking dish. Bake at 350 degrees for 30 to 35 minutes or until top springs back when touched.

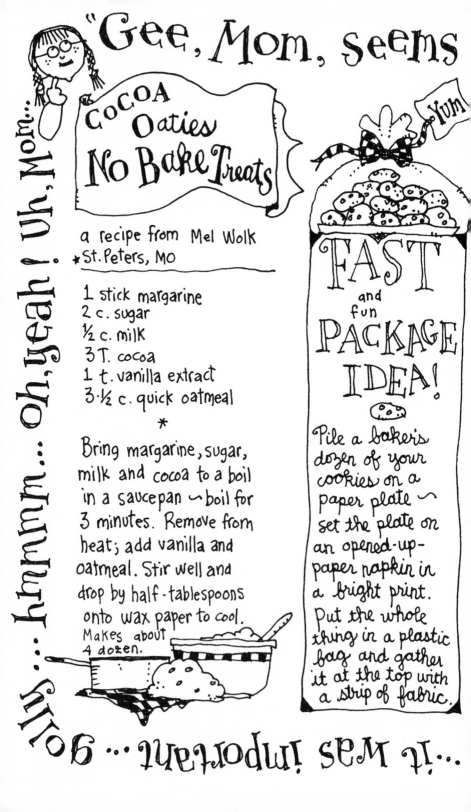

"Gee, Mom, seems

Cocoa Oaties No Bake Treats

a recipe from Mel Wolk
★ St. Peters, MO

1 stick margarine
2 c. sugar
½ c. milk
3 T. cocoa
1 t. vanilla extract
3·½ c. quick oatmeal

*

Bring margarine, sugar, milk and cocoa to a boil in a saucepan — boil for 3 minutes. Remove from heat; add vanilla and oatmeal. Stir well and drop by half-tablespoons onto wax paper to cool. Makes about 4 dozen.

Yum

FAST and fun PACKAGE IDEA!

Pile a baker's dozen of your cookies on a paper plate — set the plate on an opened-up-paper napkin in a bright print. Put the whole thing in a plastic bag and gather it at the top with a strip of fabric.

...it was important... golly... hmmm... oh, yeah! uh, Mom...

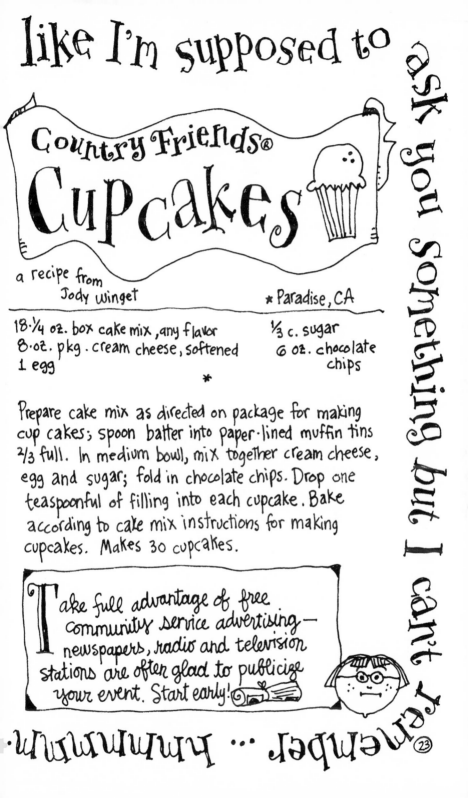

Country Friends® Cupcakes

a recipe from
Jody Winget

★ Paradise, CA

18.¼ oz. box cake mix, any flavor
8 oz. pkg. cream cheese, softened
1 egg

⅓ c. sugar
6 oz. chocolate chips

*

Prepare cake mix as directed on package for making cupcakes; spoon batter into paper-lined muffin tins ⅔ full. In medium bowl, mix together cream cheese, egg and sugar; fold in chocolate chips. Drop one teaspoonful of filling into each cupcake. Bake according to cake mix instructions for making cupcakes. Makes 30 cupcakes.

Take full advantage of free community service advertising— newspapers, radio and television stations are often glad to publicize your event. Start early!

Kate's ⋆ Gotta ⋆ Have ⋆ It ⋆ Now
Seven ⋆ Layer ⋆ Bars

"I think that I shall never eat, nuthin' good as this here treat."

a recipe from Carolyn Hatch ⋆ Salinas, CA

½ c. butter, melted
1·¼ c. graham cracker crumbs
1 c. flaked coconut
6-oz. pkg. chocolate chips

3 oz. butterscotch chips
1 c. chopped nuts
14-oz. can sweetened condensed milk

⋆

Combine butter and graham cracker crumbs; spread mixture in a 13" x 9" baking pan. Layer remaining ingredients on in the order listed. Bake at 350 degrees for 25 to 30 minutes. Cool for 15 minutes before cutting into bars.

BAKE SALE TODAY

A poet should be read and not seen.
—C. DAY LEWIS

24

Pumpkin Cheesecake Bars

a recipe from
Kim Henry

★ Library, PA

16-oz. box pound cake mix
3 eggs, divided
2 T. margarine, melted
4 t. pumpkin pie spice, divided
8-oz. pkg. cream cheese

14-oz. can sweetened
condensed milk
16-oz. can pumpkin
½ t. salt

*

In large bowl, combine cake mix, one egg, margarine and 2 t. pumpkin pie spice on low speed 'til crumbly. Press into bottom of a jelly roll pan; set aside. Blend cream cheese until fluffy; beat in condensed milk, pumpkin, salt, remaining eggs and pie spice. Pour over crust and bake at 350 degrees for 30 to 40 minutes. Cool and cut into bars. Makes 22 to 24 bars.

COOKIES

3 for $1.00
homemade!

It is not where you serve, but how you serve.

∽ J. RUBIN CLARK

UH, SO SORRY...ALL GONE... NONE LEFT... TRY AGAIN NEXT YEAR!

CARAMEL APPLE PIES HERE

Caramel Apple Pie

...don't neglect to share!

a recipe from Paula Lyon ★ Shawnee, OK

10 caramel candies, quartered
1/3 c. all-purpose flour
3 c. apples, chopped

2/3 c. caramel ice cream topping
2 t. lemon juice
1/2 c. pecan pieces
9" pie crust

Combine caramels and flour; blend in apples, caramel topping and lemon juice; mix well. Pour into 9" pie crust and sprinkle with pecan pieces. Bake at 375 degrees for 40 to 45 minutes.

Chocolate Dream Pie

a recipe from Jeannie Craig ★ Charlotte, NC

3 eggs
1.1/2 c. sugar
1 stick butter
2 sq. unsweetened chocolate

2 t. vanilla extract
13 oz. can evaporated milk, warmed
9" deep dish pie crust

Beat eggs 'til light—add sugar and beat well. Melt butter and chocolate over low heat, add to eggs. Add milk and vanilla. Pour into 9" deep dish pastry shell greased well with margarine. Bake at 425° for 25 minutes.

oh·so Peachy Tart

a recipe from
Susan Fratanduono ★ Newark Valley, NY

4 to 6 peaches, peeled and sliced
9" pie crust
1 c. sugar   2 T. all-purpose flour
2 eggs   2 T. butter, melted

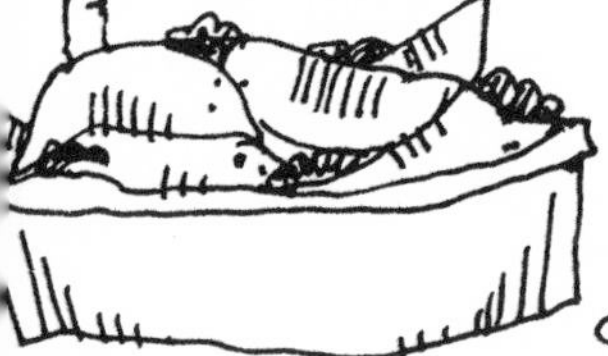

Spoon peaches into pie crust; set aside.
Mix sugar, eggs and flour together.
Slowly add melted butter and blend.
Pour over peaches. Bake at 350 degrees for 50 to 60 minutes.

♥ **Charity** ♥
begins
at home,
but should
not end
there.
—THOMAS
FULLER·

Pies and tarts are great sellers at a bake sale
but sometimes are so juicy, they're hard to
cut up into single servings. Some ideas:

★ Sell the pie as a whole. You can't beat those nice,
disposable foil pans for ease ~ but you can dress the
pan up a little! Wrap the whole thing in food-safe
decorative cellophane or mylar with the wrap gathered
at the top with a ribbon or pretty trim ~ a
silk daisy glued on a chocolate pie perhaps.

★ Experiment making small versions of
your pie in muffin pans or cupcake liners.

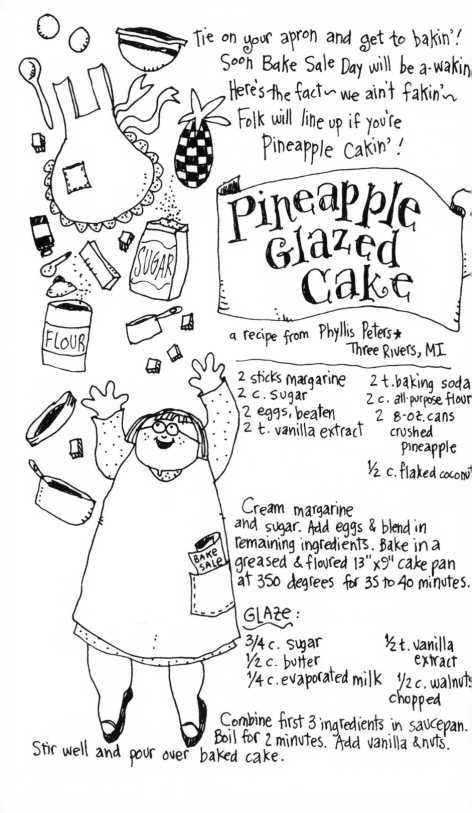

Tie on your apron and get to bakin'!
Soon Bake Sale Day will be a-wakin'
Here's the fact~ we ain't fakin'~
Folk will line up if you're
Pineapple Cakin'!

Pineapple Glazed Cake

a recipe from Phyllis Peters⋆
Three Rivers, MI

2 sticks margarine
2 c. sugar
2 eggs, beaten
2 t. vanilla extract

2 t. baking soda
2 c. all-purpose flour
2 8-oz. cans
  crushed
    pineapple

½ c. flaked coconut

Cream margarine
and sugar. Add eggs & blend in
remaining ingredients. Bake in a
greased & floured 13"x9" cake pan
at 350 degrees for 35 to 40 minutes.

GLAZE:

3/4 c. sugar
½ c. butter
¼ c. evaporated milk

½ t. vanilla
  extract
½ c. walnuts
  chopped

Combine first 3 ingredients in saucepan.
Boil for 2 minutes. Add vanilla & nuts.
Stir well and pour over baked cake.

3 is your lucky number!

"Three" Chocolate Cake

a recipe from LuAnn Williams
★New Tripoli, PA

3 c. all-purpose flour
3 c. sugar
3 eggs
3/4 c. cocoa
3 t. baking powder
3 t. baking soda
3/4 c. vegetable oil
3 c. boiling water

Mix first 7 ingredients together. Add hot water and mix for 2 minutes. Pour batter into a greased 13"x 9" baking pan. Bake at 350 degrees for 40 to 45 minutes.

Decisions, Decisions!

Bundt

Fudge Marble ♥

cherry 5 layer

Pineapple Glazed ♥

Uh, yes, hello, I'm from the Health Department. I will need to confiscate your first batch of Bake Sale Toffee for possible, uh, weevil contamination. There is a serious outbreak of, um, weevilitis in this area and I need to....

Good homemade candy is a real treat for those sweet-toothers who don't have time or talent in the kitchen... So sell 'em!

See my friend over there? (DON'T LOOK!) She's going to try to con you into letting her have first shot at your toffee. It's a sham. Now, I, on the other hand ...

Please. I'm begging you. Make this recipe for your next bake sale. I will surely expire if I don't get it. I'm feeling faint. I probably need sugar. Yeah, low blood sugar, that's it. I need it now. Better make a sample batch immediately. Call me. I'll come over and test it for you. Night or day. I'm not kidding. After all, it's a charity thing, am I right? Do I look pale to you? My doctor says.

BAKE·SALE·TOFFEE

a recipe from Mona Royer ★ Houston, TX

1 lb. butter
2 c. sugar
2 t. corn syrup
¼ t. salt
4 4-oz. pkgs. slivered almonds
¼ t. baking soda
12-oz. pkg. chocolate chips

Melt butter in saucepan ⁓ add sugar. Over medium heat, add corn syrup, salt & nuts. Stir constantly until candy thermometer reaches 310 degrees. Remove from heat and add baking soda. Spread on 2 greased cookie sheets ⁓ flatten very thin with back of spatula. Melt chocolate chips in double-boiler 'til smooth, then spread over toffee. Cool completely ⁓ break into pieces.

Pecan Pie ♥ Mini Muffins

a recipe from Kathy Mentink
★ Elgin, IL

1 c. brown sugar, packed
½ c. all-purpose flour
1 c. pecans, chopped
2/3 c. butter, melted
2 eggs, beaten

*

In a bowl, combine first three ingredients; set aside. Combine butter & eggs — mix well. Stir into flour mixture until just moistened. Fill greased & floured or paper-lined miniature muffin cups 2/3 full. Bake at 350 degrees for 20 to 25 minutes or until tested done. Remove immediately to cool on wire racks. Makes 2½ dozen muffins.

YUM!

an IDEA:

Sell a "SAMPLER PLATE" ～
three or four cookies, a yummy muffin and a slice of cake ～ just for those who can't decide!

"Between 2 evils, I always pick the one I never tried before. — MAE WEST

Set a monetary goal for your bake sale — it will give you a target to aim for!

Aim high!

Index

country friends®

Bake Sale Today!